ANIMAL RIGHTS:
PEDIGREE OR AESTHETICS

Dr. Paul R. Friesen

2021

https://www.vox.com/the-highlight/22369273/frenchie-doodle-designer-dogsproblems-breeder-shelter

https://sites.google.com/view/3dlearninganimalrights/home

Animal Rights:

Title – Animal Rights: Pedigree or Aesthetics

ISBN - 978-1-716-04582-0

Author – Dr. Paul R. Friesen

Copyright – Dr. Paul R. Friesen

Publisher – www.lulu.com

Story cover pages – MS Office Templates Design

and Content – Dr. Paul R. Friesen 2021

Animal Rights:

Contents

(Quizzes are included at the end of each story. There are two (2) – True and False / Comprehension. They are uploaded if an interactive style is preferred.)

Animal Rights:

Disclaimer – *All rights for the original story go to the author and original publisher. The following is a rewrite of an article from the above URL. There is no guarantee the article is maintained on the page.*

Discovery

This section discovers what is known and what information needs to be expanded.

- Building a larger umbrella to cover the topic allows the door of critical thinking to open and the size of the umbrella to enlarge.

- Developing an argument requires a focus of information to base the initial statement on yet broad enough to push the idea into current thought and culture.

- The DISCOVERY phase requires students to present what they know. With a guide, this discovery is expanded to include a broader range of ideas. The initial discussion will be used later as building blocks for exploration and reference.

- Building blocks come from ideas generated from discovery. Teams use blocks of information to tie the defense of the argument together.

- Students require attentiveness to take notes at every stage of preparation. These notes are constantly reviewed and challenged by the team.

- The team, consisting of several people, builds blocks of information to be tied to all other information for both defense and rebuttal. It is imperative to not note there is never too much information. The challenge, however, is to keep this large amount of information organized for quick review and rebuttal.

- Reading Titles for information speeds research allowing specific information to be found quickly and stored in a file folder.

- DISCOVERY is where the mass of ideas is flushed out and discussed without barriers requiring strong brainstorming skills. It is at this point the foundation that is made to support the statement.

- In this book, you will find the initial story provides the base point. In other arguments, the statement may come first. This would assume an initial level of critical thinking; Therefore, the story is the whetstone for development.

- Skills developed and used in the DISCOVERY phase are notetaking, question asking, critical thinking, reading, and speaking.

Animal Rights:

(Video 1 end) (Video 2 begin)

What can you know from the title?

Discovery is about gleaning information from the smallest of inputs. The title is the smallest input but stands as the entrance to a longer path. At this point, a person decides to pursue the fuller story or move on.

Choosing to move on will be the impetus to the discussion. Discovering how to search for relevant information will lead to better understanding and discussion.

The following statements are given to begin the generation of ideas. Add a few more to the list.

)()()()()(

Title: The very cute, totally disturbing tale of the American "it" dog

① It is about dogs.

② People are crazy about special traits.

③ It is about American / Canadian / European dogs.

④ It is about people traveling with dogs.

What do *I* know about this topic?

Check which ones are ***true for you*** and add a few more.

o Nothing!
o I love dogs.
o People go crazy about dogs.
o It is only in American.

① ____

② ____

③ ____

④ ____

)()()()()(

During the discovery of new information, whet the appetite and explore ideas about motivation, goals of the story, plus and minuses, general interest discussion. Notetaking will create a strong foundation to expand later.

What would make me buy something made just for me?

① ____

② ____

③ ____

④ ____

)()()()()(

Have you ever wanted something special in a pet?

- o   No! Why not?
- o   Yes! What did you wish for, and why?

____

____

____

Separate your ideas into groups that you think may generate information for an argument.

Examples: Selfish   */ Business*   */ Psychology*   */ Economics*
_______________ / _______________ / _______________ / _______________

Having created ideas and discussion notes about the topic read the story fitting the ideas into your 'groups of possible arguments' list.

Follow the steps outlined below. A list of words you may not know is given. Add more information to each to enable your understanding.

Group work – If this is a class divide them into groups to focus on each of the five paragraphs. Have students share their ideas for **discussion**.

)()()()()(

In this section, reading, followed by critical thinking, will develop quicker outlines and build vocabulary.

A list of possible vocabulary ideas will be given. Try to make definitions without a dictionary. This is important because when preparing for a debate grasping information quickly is crucial.
(Video 1 end) (Video 2 begin)

Animal Rights:

Deciding which words have value and which create conflict in presentation without a dictionary will develop stronger English comprehension skills to be used in the debate.

① **Read the story**. This is a story rewritten for copyright protection with a URL for further review.

② Create an outline of the story/paragraphs. Long outlines seem tedious but will save you time when referencing in a timed debate setting.

③ Words that follow the story should be used in your outline. Using vocabulary in your outlines will strengthen the continued use of them. They are also good to fall back on when making your point.

)( )( )( )( )(

Tove K. Danovich

Title: *The very cute, totally disturbing tale of the American "it" dog*

[1] One of the most popular dog breeds is the French Bulldog. It is often referred to as the **"It"** breed. With **squat** figures, flat noses, and bat ears they are perfect for carryon luggage when traveling. They are best suited for lazy owners because they don't need a lot of exercise because of health issues.

[2] These trendy small dogs have been bred to accommodate their owners, not the other way around. **Housetraining** the breed to urinate on pads in a specific area is easy. **Frenchies**, as they are lovingly called, are the most '**hashtagged**' dog on Instagram. Demand for the breed has skyrocketed and even stimulating robberies, like Lady Gaga's **dog walker**.

[3] With large heads at birth, the cost of a **C-section** is almost the norm. The breed is **prone** to many health problems like infections because they are considered a **brachycephalic** breed. This means they have to pant to cool off being susceptible to heat trauma. Other issues include spine deformation and nerve pain.

[4] Many puppy mills produce large litters without caring for adult dogs. These profit from the demand, while others are more specific in their breeding to meet their clients' requests. People prefer to have pets that say "pay attention to me" through their faces and body shape. The **appeal** is usually self-oriented and not aesthetic.

[5] This breed is also famous for its **vocalizing** or **mimick**ing in an almost human voice. Owners project themselves onto their dogs not caring to listen to them. Want-to-be owners often contact **rescues** before they settle on a breed. Choosing a Frenchie makes them feel they have achieved a place in high society.

[6] Movies and animations often create a **craze** for specific breeds. One such breed was the Dalmatian. A predictable consequence of this the puppies **wind up in** a shelter. Dogs in movies are not the same as real flesh and blood ones.

[7] **Social media must also take some blame. A butt obsession propelled the waddling** Corgi into the limelight. Other popular breeds like **pugs** are famous for their flat noses while suffering from breathing issues related to them. Aspiring owners need to be aware of the high cost of maintaining the breed. As with most forced changes to a breed the quality of life long-term, health issues only get worse. The more **prestigious** the breed, the more problems arise.

[8] Some say a **brace** of Afghan Hounds was in Noah's Ark. Though we will never know, each pure breed has its origins which can be traced to Victorian England when dogs were bred for the purpose. **Studbooks** were kept and then closed to new breeds in the 1800s. Later the value increased when the dogs could be proven to be linked to the original.

[9] We have now **commodified** them for owners who want life their way and have the finances to fulfill it. One of these is a designer breed, the Labradoodle. Though the gimmick was its non-allergenic value, no one wanted them at first.

[10] Now everyone is wanting to get **on the bandwagon**. Breeding for traits has increased with movie series like "Game of Thrones". Bred for looks, health issues are overlooked and the sound of **wheezing**, snoring, and panting are considered normal for the breed.

)()()()()(

Vocabulary is where many students struggle to grasp the story. They are seen as an inhibitor rather than a building block. In the following exercises, there are two ideas to focus on. The first is the link the words have in the story. The second is an expansion to different words and how a change would affect the understanding of the story.

As a prelude to the discussion section, it is key to make groups engaging with the story on these two levels. This connection will strengthen the arguments you make and build a foundation on which to build your arguments.

)()()()()(

Animal Rights:

Vocabulary

Superscript *numbers in front of the words indicate the paragraph they are in. This makes for easy reference in the article together with bold highlights.*

[1] "It" – Breeds that are designed for specific people or traits.

[1] squat – This does not mean sit. It means short in stature.

[2] Housetraining – This is what you do for animals that live indoors.

[2] Frenchies – A breed of dog

[2] hashtagged' – This is what you use on Instagram to make comments.

[2] dogwalker – A person who walks dogs as a job or just for fun.

[3] C-section – This is a procedure for when there are issues when birthing.

[3] prone – This means something is about to happen, or a person does something almost without thinking.

[3] brachycephalic – This is a big-headed breed.

[4] puppy mills – A business that produces puppies without any care for the female which must bear the stress of birthing them.

[4] appeal – Something that stimulates a response, often emotional.

[5] vocalizing – A sound that is almost human in nature.

[5] mimic – To copy something- like a noise or action.

[5] rescues – Places where animals are taken to heal or to wait for rehoming.

[6] craze – Super hot trends.

[6] wind up in – Refers to an end point of something.

[7] obsession – To have an intense focus one item or person.

[7] propel – To throw forward or accelerate movement.

[7] waddling – Swinging your hips side to side.

[7] pugs – This is a special breed of dog with a flat nose.

[7] prestigious – This implies a well-known or powerful positioned person/item.

[8] brace – This has many meanings, but here it is a trial or race for hounds.

[8] studbooks - Stud refers to males who are valued for their traits. Books are the lists of traits, winnings, and prices to pay to sire more of the same.

[9] commodified – The idea of making an object into a tradeable commodity.

[10] on the bandwagon -This means you give your full support behind an idea.

[10] wheezing – This is a sound that is made when you can't breathe.

)()()()()(

Discovery

Ideas have been generated and strong links to the story made. As you outline use the following to revisit the discoveries you have made.

What do I know about this topic?

✱ List at least four (4) **different** ideas you have found in this story about the breeding for pleasure and animal rights. Add more from your group.

❖   Use them when you make your outline.
❖   Look at your answers, under Discussion, and fill it out to reflect the new ideas.
❖   These new ideas will help you form your debate ideas better. **Use the lines below.**

① ____
② ____
③ ____
④ ____
⑤ ____

)()()()()(

Animal Rights:

Discovery Outline

Use ideas generated above to choose the main point you will focus on.

Main topic____

- ❖ Find **_one_** (1) **_key idea_** in each paragraph. (3-5 words)
- ❖ Limiting the words helps stay focused and understand the flow of the story.

Paragraph 1 ____

Paragraph 2 ____

Paragraph 3 ____

Paragraph 4 ____

Paragraph 5 ____

Paragraph 6 ____

Paragraph 7 ____

Paragraph 8 ____

Paragraph 9 ____

Paragraph 10 ____

)-()-()-()-(

- ❖ Using complete phrases or sentences expand your point from the paragraph (word (s)).

- ❖ If you have more than 2 that is great and you should list them.

- ❖ Do not limit the ideas as you will need them later to prep for the debate.

)-()-()-()-(

❖ Expand *two things* about the ideas.

    A. ____ Paragraph 1

    B. ____

    A. ____ Paragraph 2

    B. ____

    A. ____ Paragraph 3

    B. ____

    A. ____ Paragraph 4

    B. ____

    A. ____ Paragraph 5

    A. ____

    A. ____

    B. ____

❌❌❌❌❌

❖ **Write out** your paragraphs using your previous work. Add one rebuttal paragraph for each point.

❖ **Reference each point you make**. This will make your argument stronger.

❖ Use MS Word to insert or create a reference list.

❌❌❌❌❌

❖ In the introduction use the 10 paragraph ideas to communicate the order ofyour argument/essay.

❖ In the conclusion, you repeat what you have said about the points of eachparagraph.

❌❌❌❌❌

(Video 4 end) (Video 5 begin)

Animal Rights:

Discussion

There are 3 levels of discussion. Each level is progressively more challenging. Encourage students to follow the formula (1+3+2+1). One 7-word answer as a statement followed by 3 sentences to support it. Add two more 7-word sentences to build ideas for the next question.

Continue this pattern until each level is complete. Encourage students to take notes of the ideas as they work through the answers. Do NOT let students do less than the formula, but encourage more information as backup information later on.

Encourage disagreements with a retort to **make statements about facts, not assumptions**. When assumptions are made, they should be challenged and rebutted. This builds energy and excitement, not only for the debate but also for the development of the argument.

)()()()(

Level I

① Are these the only dogs in a show? Explain.

② What traits would you like in an animal/bird/reptile?

③ Would you buy a specially bred dog? Why or why not?

④ What breed of dog would you choose - if you could?

Level II

① What is the most prestigious item you have ever owned?

② What breeds make you nervous?

③ Have you ever had a pet? What kind, when, etc.

④ What breed is most popular in your country?

Level III

① What can we learn from this story?

② Is this phenomenon a problem / becoming a problem in today's society? Explain.

③ Should we ban breeds that have excessive health issues? Explain.

④ How do we change the culture to prefer breeds with better traits?

⑤ What social problems can we see mirrored in this story?

⑥ How can we stop this craze for specialty breeds from happening in our society?

)()()()()(

(Video 5 end) (Video 6 Begin)

Discussion Graphic

❖ In the first graphic students will make statements about the main topic they chose earlier.

❖ A sample is in the book. Make sure you make 1 for each person on the team.

❖ This is important because, though you are a team, the debate will be individual arguments. Coordination of all the information is crucial to this final goal.

❖ Information is always changeable.

)()()()()(

Question ~ Is requesting traits that inhibit health in a pet abuse of privilege or a right of ownership in society?

Answer ~ I think owning is a ______ and any special breeding is ….

☆ **Privilege is** one of the key ideas and is general enough to use for discussion. Understanding the idea of privilege and how we use it today allows the development of the topic from the past to the present.

☆☆ When developing an argument, ideas need to **transcend time as the idea may be the same but the object may have change**d. When researching for common elements consider this.

Animal Rights:

Make a graphic to help this process. A sample has been started. Fill the rest in as the team works on this topic. **Each team should have a separate topic and develop their graph.**

In the **first** row of the graph, you find **_key talking points_** to focus on. This defines **privilege** and allows for the expansion of the idea. This answers the question – Why do we **require special traits that are harmful**?

In the **second** row, the opposing team will state their point as 'against'.

In the **third** row, the first team will refute the 'against' point and **add more support** for their initial point.

)()()()(

Make a similar graph on a blank sheet of paper assigning one team member to each point in the first row. Make the graph large enough to accommodate all team members.

This is the first point to work with. There should be at least one major point for each team to manage. A team is defined as more than one person so it will depend on the size of the debate group.

Writing out your discussion graph enables a better view and gives precise directions. This makes **researching material-efficient** which is key to regrouping when in the debate itself.

)()()()(

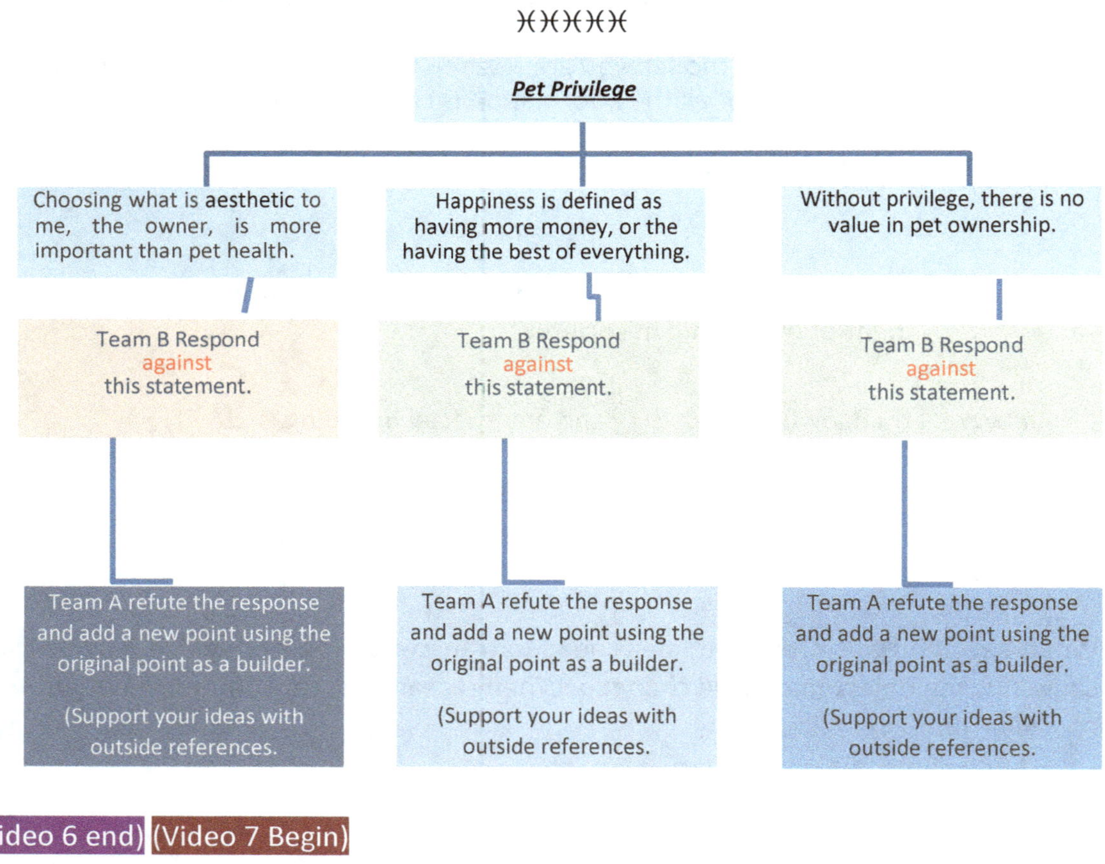

(Video 6 end) (Video 7 Begin)

The Debate

In debate, you will have a ***statement, not a question***. You have to react to the statement with facts, not opinions, and defend with specific information about your **position (for/against)**.

'Position' is understood to be either to **support** the statement or **oppose** the statement.

Both positions need to be ***researched*** with proper sentence structures and vocabulary. Vocabulary comes from research and a notebook should be kept up-to-date for the whole team to use.

There is topic-related and general use vocabulary. For this story, general use vocabulary is located at the end of the idea and may be added to include other words found during research. It is important the team understands the vocabulary and its use to better support or rebut their argument position. Being able to function well with both requires extensive practice.

❖ **Discussions** are based *on **opinions** and **answers** to **questions***. This is where these two ideas, though similar, are different.

❖ ***Debate is about*** *facts **and** *statements*.

)()()()(

When you make a statement from a story, you must consider what the core issue is. If you have made a good outline, you will have discovered this already.

This story is from economics and the core issue could be;

❖ Social
❖ Economic
❖ Political
❖ Culture.

Today the topics could range from;

❖ Abuse
❖ Rights
❖ Environment
❖ Privilege
❖ Health
❖ Economics.

These are all good arguments you would want to research for your argument.

)()()()(

Animal Rights:

Debate Statement

The debate statement can be the most difficult choice. It is the focus of the argument and should be as precise as possible. Below are a few to choose from, or make your own through discussion with the team.

The danger is to make a statement that is too long. Too much information in the statement creates a focal point that is too narrow. Stick to the key issue you want to debate. Remember the purpose of the debate is to build the argument starting from "Why?". 'Why' is a difficult question to answer and therefore the first effort should be here. Once you have determined the "Why?" you can find facts to support your idea.

- ❖ The designer pet trend is based on greed, a product of human nature, and nobody will stop it.

- ❖ Puppy mill pets feed the greed while creating a surge of rescue shelters.

- ❖ Designer pets should not be allowed because it leads to shorter lifespans and diminishing quality of life.

    Your team idea - ____

    ____

ⵣⵣⵣⵣ

(Video 7 end) (Video 8 begin)

Before you start choose one of the above statements. Then decide which position you will defend; **'for'** or '_against_'.

- ✓ Research to find FACTS for your position.
- ✓ List the facts.
- ✓ Write your argument in a long paragraph format.
- ✓ Include the opposite position in your writing.

✹ ✹ You need to write both sides so you can understand the other sides' argument.

This is the end of the discovery and discussion sections. From this point, you will need to review the story and search the Internet for more ideas.

Make a reference for each extra story researched. you can do this easily in MS Word by using the REFERENCE tab on the top ribbon. You fill in the blanks and the program will add the information at the end of the page or paper.

* This is important when moving to the debate or you can be challenged about the data you present.

* This is important because the other team will search and find the same material for their side of the argument.

* This is important because you need more than one story to make an argument and you need to match the argument with your statement.

Graphic Organization

Brainstorming is crucial in the process of preparing for the debate. When you develop the organization, test it on your teammates. If your group is large, making them smaller with specific tasks would help. In the following graphic organizer use five (5) paragraphs to put your ideas into. Though the story has ten (10), compress them into five key ideas. This will enable a large enough task for each group.

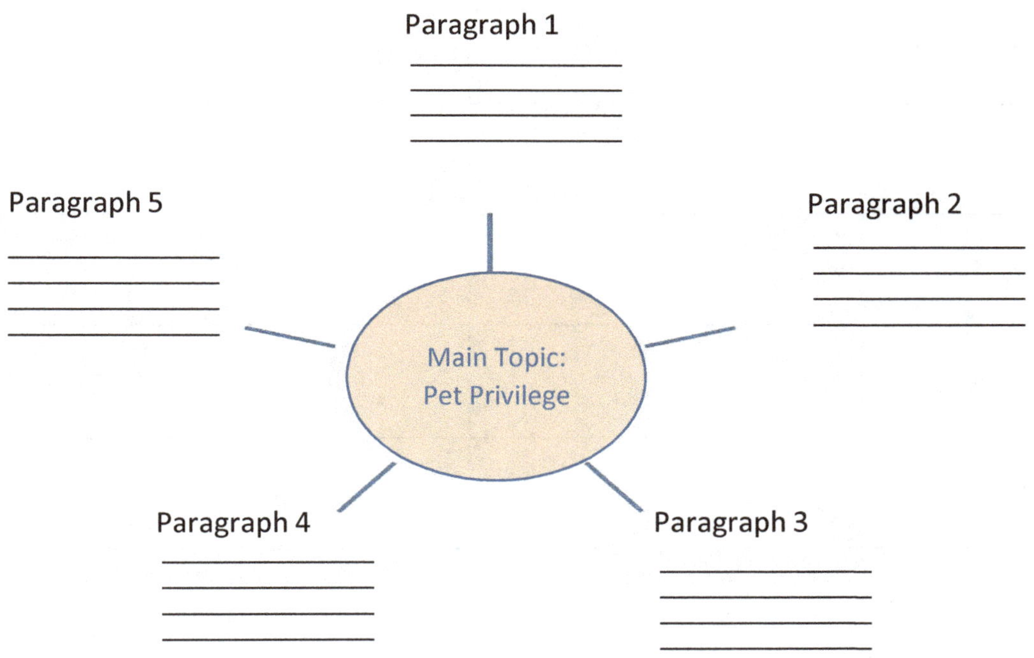

)()()()()(

Paragraph 1

Paragraph 5

Paragraph 2

Main Topic:
Pet Privilege

Paragraph 4

Paragraph 3

Write your statement here --

)()()()()(

Animal Rights:

To make your argument you should understand the connections. In the next chart list your argument facts and ideas.

(Video 8 end) (Video 9 begin)

Facts

For   Against

- Add more if needed

For	Against
1.	
2.	
3.	
4.	
5.	
6.	
7.	
8.	
9.	
10.	

Arguments do not work well in reverse. This means it must constantly move forward. In English, this can be done using the – If-Then idea.

)()()()(

Using the graphic organization ideas, you made before make a graphic using the if-then connection. Understanding this as a constant will enable more efficient answers.

Often confusion and stress come from not being able to finish the 'then' in the sequence. Answering as many if-then sequences throughout the development will create strength in the rebuttal and response.

The debate practice is about to begin. Is the team ready? Is the statement understood correctly? What side issues are there which are not connected but may be brought up.

Many points may be made but most are not relevant to the statement or argument. The team must be ready for these to refute and bring the argument back to the core point.

)(

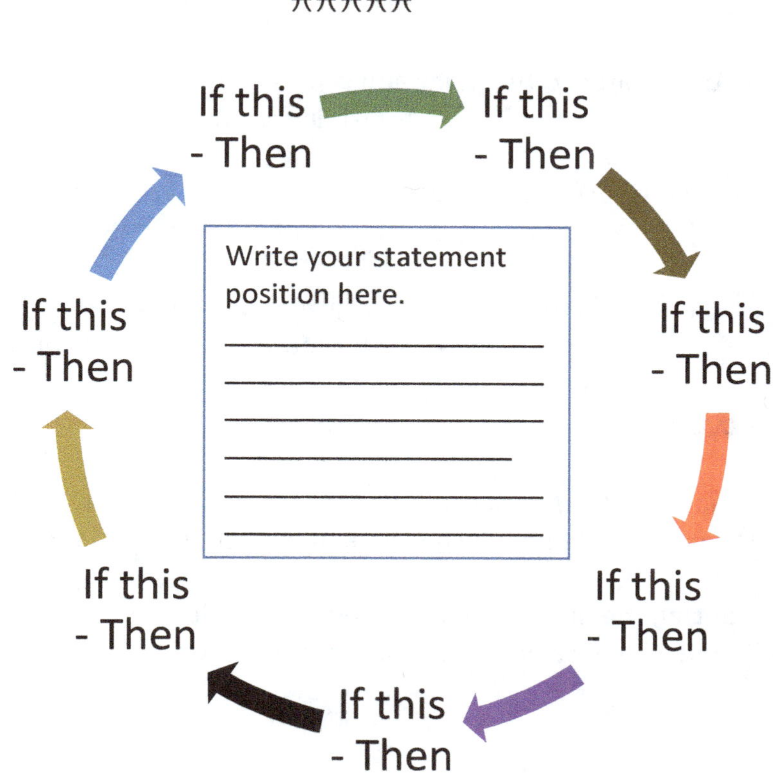

(Video 9 end) (Video 10 begin)

Animal Rights:

Get Ready to DEBATE

- ✓ The statement has already been decided and agreed to.
- ✓ Set the teams.
- ✓ Choose the position each side will defend.
- ✓ As a team, choose which point each person or team will present.
- ✓ Each person will listen for the opposite point and create a new response to what the other person has presented.

Most debates allow for one (1) presentation from each team member initially. This will be followed by a rebuttal in which specific points can be addressed with the rebuttal presented by the person who has the information at hand.

A: Point 1 (3 minutes)

Opposing Team, A: responds to the point and gives a new point.
(1-minute rebuttal) (3 minutes)

B: Rebuts the point and gives a new point.
(1-minute rebuttal) (3 minutes)

Opposing Team, A: responds to the point and gives a new point.
(1-minute rebuttal) (3 minutes)

Continue the cycle.

After all persons have spoken, each can respond to any point given by the opposite team, or add more points from their team which will need a response from the opposite team.

Following the rebuttal, the public will be invited to ask relevant questions. The questions will be team-specific with the answer given by a spokesperson.

)()()()()(

Date of the debate ______________________

Where is the debate held?   ______________________

What time is the debate to be held ______________________

Team names ______________________

Judges ______________________

Statement to defend ______________________

Animal Rights:

Dear Teacher/ Student,

This is only part of a curriculum. Challenging the status quo is important for students to discover and explore new ideas. Moving out of a personal comfort zone heightens the motivation to take risks.

Creating this challenge through debate builds a better foundation for any future job or discussion. It is not helpful to poke eyes out only, but it is useful to understand why the blindness and have a solution to stop the problem.

Going beyond is the expansion into essay writing. Good essays can build and defend an argument. Building a structure for debate will springboard off this skill set.

Professor Paul R. Friesen
2021

Quizzes

based on the vocabulary and story

Animal Rights:

QUIZ 1 (NON-interactive)

Fill in the blanks with the correct word(s) found in the box.

1. C-Sections are __________

   inexpensive. outrageous, cheap, expensive

2. The Frenchie breed is ________ to breathing problems.

   prone / C-section / hashtagged / expensive / puppy mills

3. _____________ produce large litters without caring about the dog.

   Paper mills / Puppy mills / Rescues / Frenchies

4. The ______ of these dogs is not the aesthetics.

   sex / color / weight / appeal

5. Frenchie's are famous for _______ their owners.

   rescue / craze / mimicking / winding up

6. This breed is famous for its flat nose. ______

   Pug / Frenchie/ Afghan / Shepherd

7. The more __________ the more problems arise.

   money / prestigious / waddling / propel

8. Most specially bred dogs __________________ in a shelter.

   wind up / die / get sick / get fed up

9. A brace of hounds refers to ________________.

   a trial / rabbit chasing / dogs and cats/ all of the above

10. These were used to keep a log of pedigree. _____________.

    Money bags / Studbooks / Study books / E-books

)()()()()(

<u>Quiz 1</u> (Interactive)

This is an interactive quiz. Send this to students to do on their phone or computer. Click on the line, then on the arrow on the right to find your answer choices.

1. C-Sections are __________ .

2. The Frenchie breed is __________ to breathing problems.

3. __________ produce large litters without caring about the dog.

4. *The* __________ of these dogs is not the aesthetics.

5. Frenchie's are famous for __________ their owners.

6. This breed is famous for its flat nose. __________

7. The more __________ the more problems arise.

8. Most specially bred dogs __________ in a shelter.

9. A brace of hounds refers to __________ .

10. These were used to keep a log for pedigree __________ .

)()()()(

Animal Rights:

Quiz 2 (Interactive)

*Send this to students to do on their phone or computer and return it with their name or email on it. Click on the line, then the arrow on the right to find your answer choices. **Or,** print and have them fill it out with T or F.*

True / False

1. The 'It' breed refers to only the Frenchie. [1] T / F (____)

2. When a dog is bred for show it is brachycephalic [3] T / F (____)

3. Poodles are the most 'hashtagged' on google [2] T / F (____)

4. Rescues are places you can train your dog to sit. [5] T / F (____)

5. Craze means you are insane. [6] T / F (____)

6. Waddling is to shake your but from side to side. [7] T / F (____)

7. When something is commodified it becomes a commodity. [9] T / F (____)

8. When you are on the bandwagon you play guitar. [10] T / F (____)

9. Wheezing indicates you are tired. [10] T / F (____)

10. When you have an obsession, you love perfume. [7] T / F (____)

)()()()(

Answers for Quiz 1

1. expensive 2. prone 3. Puppy mills 4. appeal 5. mimicking 6. Pug

7. prestigious 8. wind up 9. trial 10. Studbooks

Answers for Quiz 2

1. False 2. False 3. False 4. False 5. False 6. True 7. True 8. False

9. False 10. False

✂✂✂✂✂

✂ All quizzes are on the homepage for easy reference and sending to students.

https://sites.google.com/view/3dlearninganimalrights/quizzes

Animal Rights:

Extra Vocabulary

These words can be found in the original story. The definitions are the authors.

Paragraph numbers refer to the original story. Please **review the original** as you prepare for the debate.

1. cognition – This refers to what and how a dog understands us. [7]

2. vocalize – To make sounds or mimic sounds. [7]

3. fawn – This is to give special attention to something. [9]

4. crave – To have an intense desire for something. [10]

5. standing out – Be different than your surroundings so you are noticed. [10]

6. litter – The name used for animals who have more than one offspring. [11]

7. predictable consequence – To tell the future from an event. [13]

8. aspirational – To aspire is to dream of better things. [15]

9. Labradoodle – A cross breed of Labrador and poodle. [24]

10. gimmick – A little something to encourage participation or sale. [24]

11. crossbreed – This is what they call animals which are bred for specific purposes. [24]

12. trait – A special characteristic of something. [26]

13. metastasized – A process of change which affects the whole. [26]

14. in-group – A select group of people which is the jealousy of many. [27]

15. whippet – A breed of dog descending from the greyhound. [30]

16. cropped ears – Ears that are cut to a specific shape. [36]

17. docked tails – Tails that are cut short for style and looks. [36]

Animal Rights:

Other topics in the series

10 Debatable Topics to use in Flipped Learning Classes – ISBN **9-781-7947-0899-0**
https://www.lulu.com/en/us/shop/paul-r-friesen/10-debatable-topics-for-flipped-learning-classes/paperback/product-p85222.html

Business: Big companies push for profit at the expense of workers
ISBN - 9-781-716 - 04839-5

Farming: The Fix is in
ISBN - 9-781-715-04798-5

Gold: The Yukon Story
ISBN - 9-781-716-03907-2

Sports: Rescue and Risk
ISBN 9-781-716-04248-5

Sports: Tae Kwon Do
ISBN - 9-781-716-04274-4

Environment: Mining and Pollution
ISBN 9-781-716-04201-0

Food: Milk and Honey
ISBN - 9-781-716-03874-7

Animal Rights: Pedigree or Aesthetics
ISBN - 9-781-716-045822-0

Economics: Equality at Whose Expense? - Unfair but more efficient
ISBN - 9-781-716-04216-4

Art: Whose is it Really?
ISBN - 9-781-1-716-03818-1

Dr. Paul R. Friesen has been in the ESL field for over 20 years. He published his first ESL book in 2010, *Making Conversation Work For You*. He has also written papers on ideas like the 7AIQ method of engaging in dialogue with better results. He is currently developing the formula 1+3+2+Q which expands on that theory. These stories are not about the debate, the end activity, but interacting with what the student reads more critically. Enjoy them as an individual or as a group with a teacher. Take up the challenge.

978-1-716-04582-0
Imprint: Lulu.com

Suggested Retail 12.95 USD

www.ingramcontent.com/pod-product-compliance
Lightning Source LLC
Chambersburg PA
CBHW080207250726
48657CB00008B/2492